Horse 101

Everything You Wish You Had Known Before You Got Your First Horse

(And a few chuckles for experienced horse owners)

April Love
Email: april@holistichorseworks.com
Web: holistichorseworks.com

Illustrated by Sheela K. Rose

By April Love
(formerly April Battles)

DVDs

- Level 1 Equine Musculoskeletal Unwinding Home Study Program – DVD & Workbook
- Level 2 Home Study Equine Cranio Sacral and Advanced Applied Kinesiology
- Equine Cranio Sacral Energy Work
- Canine Musculoskeletal Unwinding
- Horses with Headaches
- Horses Are Talking – Are You Listening?
- Bodywork for Foals home study

YouTube Videos

- Sore, Cranky, or Lame Horses?
- Horse Issues That Are Easy Fixes
- Free Yoga for Horses
- Cow Hocked Horses
- Evaluating Sore Horses
- Belly Lifts to Stretch Out Top Line
- Releasing Defense Postures
- Front Leg Stretches for Horses
- Why You Want to Learn How to Do Bodywork on Your Horse
- Introduction to HolisticHorseWorks
- And over 100 more.

Horse 101

Everything You Wish You Had Known Before You Got Your First Horse

April Love

Email: april@holistichorseworks.com
Web: holistichorseworks.com
Holistichorseworksclub.com
Illustrated by Sheela K. Rose

Library of Congress In-Publication Data
April Love
Horse 101
1. Nonfiction.   2. Equine.

ISBN: 9781973134060 (Paperback)

Illustrations by Sheela K. Rose

Third Edition – August 2019

Dedication

This book is dedicated to all the passionate horse lovers out there who are or have been frustrated with buying the wrong products that sounded good, but did not really help their horse get better, or spent thousands of dollars on horse training only to get back a horse that was worse, not better.

My hope is that, in a humorous way, this little book will give you insight into how to do things a bit better for your horses the first time AND save you money in the long run. Preventing an issue is way cheaper than treating an issue.

Table of Contents

Introduction

All the things you wish you had known before going into your first horse ownership.

So, if you are looking for or recently bought your first horse, here is some helpful advice. These are just my personal insights and experiences and not meant to replace any veterinary diagnostics or recommended care.

Maybe it was love at first sight. Something called to you to buy this horse. You were so smitten you might not have noticed any obvious defects a longtime horse owner would have noticed.

Your first horse

Your first horse may have come into your life because it was 'affordable,' cheap or free.

Or something inside you called out that you needed to have or save a very expensive horse that was not in good condition; perhaps without even thinking about where it was going to live or what it needed to eat. You just knew this horse needed you and you needed this horse.

No one told you about preparing for future veterinary bills, temperamental farriers, unsolicited advice from friends, and saddle-fitting issues . . . and the list goes on. You just knew you two were meant to be together—those big, brown, soft eyes that looked at you adoringly...

First off, they do not understand the concept of being owned. Moving them to a new home can be very stressful. Finding a new safe place to sleep, losing herd buddies, and having to make new friends can be very stressful to them and can upset their digestion.

Why is their digestion so important?
Well, horses have a one-way digestive tract. They cannot throw up if they have an upset tummy. They can get blockages and gas can collect, which can turn into what is called a 'colic,' meaning the gas is building. They are bloating and cannot push things through their system. They might lay down and try to roll to move things around. They can twist their

intestine which is very painful, and this would be your first expensive veterinary call.

About twenty-five years ago, before I learned all I have about taking care of horses, I fell in love with a beautiful, five-year-old, 'dapple grey' Arabian mare named Jerusha. I saw her in the cross ties at a barn where I was volunteering and had dreams about her. I could not get her out of my mind.

I had been given riding lessons starting at age ten and rode until I was seventeen; mostly bareback, meaning without a saddle. And here I was at age thirty, getting back into horses because I had found something was 'missing in my life.'

Does this sound familiar? The kids are grown and away, and as we get older, the call to have a horse in our life gets stronger: something that loves you unconditionally, doesn't nag or point out flaws, and is always glad to see you with a treat in your hand.

When I found her, it helped me to feel complete. She nickered at me when I would go visit her. Yes, she knew I always brought her carrots, which the owners never did. I was not aware that she was not 'broke.' I certainly didn't want a 'broken horse.' I wanted a fixed horse, I thought.

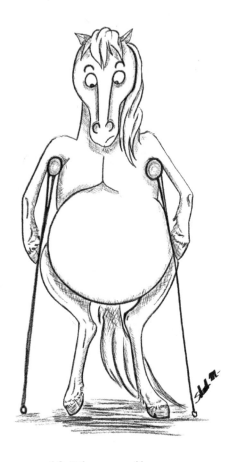

I still chuckle about that to this day. When I swung up onto her bareback, I thought the rearing up on her hind legs was because I had startled her, and the hi-ho-silver was fun. Ah, youth! Luckily, she loved me by that time, so no damage was done to her or myself. They really are amazing! They give so much from their hearts to those who are lucky enough to be loved by them.

After finishing the payments on her high price tag, which was quite high for an 'unbroke horse,' I found a place closer to my home for her. I was not aware she had never been in a horse trailer, nor away from the place where she'd been born or her mother, the dam. Usually, they're weaned from their moms at about six months of age. It's a good idea to ask the history of a horse before pulling them out of their familiar

environment.

I got her to her new place, of course, and gave her new feed. She was nervous and scared and, wham, colicked that night.

April Love

That was twenty-five years ago, before smartphones and google, so I had no way to call anyone or google anything: just a phone booth at the barn to call the woman I had bought her from. Then, lots and lots of hand walking for hours to keep her moving.

One person advised me to give her Coca-Cola; she said the carbonation would help. I was desperate and willing to try anything. Now, here I was looking at the can of coke, wondering how I was supposed to get it down her throat without wearing all the sticky mess. Hold her jaw up and pour it in her mouth? Are you kidding me? Yes, I'm sure I was wearing more than she swallowed, but we really bonded that night.

I know now that it's a good idea to make them a wet mash with soaked bran or beet pulp before and after moving them; at least for a few days. Add a teaspoon of iodized salt; preferably a natural salt. Epsom salt can work as well to help keep their gut moving in a healthy way while their digestive system gets used to the new feed they will be getting.

They really should be pooping at least five to ten times a day, if not more. No poop in their home environment is the first sign to call your local veterinarian.

I do have a YouTube video on what to do while waiting for the vet to come, which includes my yoga belly lifts and butt tucks to help the horse move the gas out of their intestines. When you combine the belly lift and butt tuck at the same time, you'll usually get a very large, long expulsion of stinky gas. So, I do not recommend standing directly behind the horse!

Getting a half to a whole bale of hay from the previous owner—what the horse was used to eating—is a smart thing to do while transitioning the horse to its new environment.

If you treat them with kindness and loving treats, they will decide that they now own you! And what is a treat? A piece of carrot, an apple or you can buy horse treats at the feed store. I prefer the more natural treats. Small pieces are best as a horse's front teeth are not designed to break a carrot in half or bite into an apple. The front teeth are designed for grazing and tearing grass. The TMJ jaw joint is not designed to break something hard using the front teeth. Always feed a treat on the flat of your hand where the horses can smell it and find it with their lips. Their lips can be very talented at picking up things. I have had some horses that could untie themselves or open the stall door to let themselves out to graze or run and play. Yes, they can be tricky and smart!

Here are some things you should know so your horse can be the best it can be to be a safe riding companion and stay rideable longer. And you'll have fewer accidents and veterinary bills.

Where to start? Nose to tail? Temperaments? Saddle fit? Nutrition? Hooves?

There's so much good advice on the Internet these days.

You could literally spend months looking at websites, YouTube videos, and Facebook pages: sources to provide you with advice on what to do for your horse.

Everyone at your barn will have their own opinion as well. Beware of the 'barn politics' as some people take offense when given advice or if you do not take their advice. And no matter how hard you try to do the right thing; someone will always tell you you're not doing it right.

So, here is my short version to get you started.

Chapter 1 - Breeds

Here's a general breakdown of breeds. Of course, there are many exceptions to the rules and many more breeds than mentioned here.

You get a big, thick-bodied horse that goes slow and is usually more reliable. These are called the **cold bloods** or **draft cross breeds**. Also, harder to spread your legs to ride. Be very careful where you place your feet, so they don't step on them.

By big-body style, we are not referring to the ones that pack away the groceries.

Then there are the more medium-build horses like the Quarter Horse, Morgan, and Welsh breeds. These horses are bred to work cattle, pull carts, and are all-around work and family horses.

For small children, the Welsh Cob breeds are a good choice. They usually have a good brain and are easy to be around. They're versatile and can carry some weight as your child gets older and bigger. Also, their resale value is usually higher when well trained.

Then there are the thin-bodied horses, called the **hot bloods**, meant for speed and covering a lot of ground such as Arabians and Thoroughbreds. These can be used for racing as well as athletic competition. By athletic, I mean they can decide to go in another direction in the blink of an eye, and if you were riding them at the time you may find the ground quite unforgiving. We call this an *involuntary dismount—* you did not choose to dismount at that time.

I used to do fifty miles in a day on my Arabian gelding in what is called **Endurance riding**—a very fun organized way to see the countryside from horseback, with marked trails and rest stops.

There's nothing like flying through the woods on your fast steed. And when you are flying through those woods, wind in your face, and a deer pops out of the bushes—something smaller than your horse—you will see just how athletic your one-thousand-pound steed can be and how fast an *involuntary dismount* can happen.

Then there are the half breeds like mules with very long ears and longer lifespans. A mule is a cross between a female horse and a male donkey or jackass. They are usually sterile, meaning not able to reproduce, and have good hooves and they generally don't need horseshoes.

I recommend, whatever breed you choose, to get an older, more experienced horse.

Sadly, I've seen first-time horse owners buy a young horse because it was very pretty running around fast with its tail in the air, that's not always the best choice for a first-time horse owner.

There are always exceptions to every breed as everything depends on the temperament and upbringing of the horse, of course. Older horses know the routine and typically have a been-there-done-that attitude. The younger ones can spook at something they haven't seen before and turn or spin out from under you, leaving you in the dirt—not intentionally— but our bones do not always take kindly to our *involuntary dismounts*.

Why do I keep mentioning this type of dismount? So you will know the possibilities and be forewarned. I found when I was young, I could bounce and get right up and get back on the horse. After age forty, I found the ground was very hard and after getting up off the ground very slowly, feeling for anything broken, x-rays were usually needed.

The best thing about getting a cheap horse was the price, and there was usually a reason why they were so affordable.

Typically, a good horse starts at $2,000 and up—the more training, the bigger the price tag, of course. Just like buying a used car—the cheaper it is, the more issues it has.

Unfortunately, most cheap horses are passed around because of 'behavior issues' or 'training issues' when, in reality, those 'issues' are pain issues in the body. We all have pain and compensation issues as we get older. Well, so do horses!

Believe it or not, horses have good and bad days just like we do. So, let's learn together how to keep them in their primarily good days.

If I can explain how to do that in a way that is easy to understand and easy to do, would this interest you?

Once you know what they really need in order to move from being in constant pain—most horses even have headaches, which can make them cranky or unsafe for family members—the rest of your partnership with them can move forward with joy and ease.

April Love

Chapter 2 - Things to Consider

So, what do you want to do with your horse? Do you want to ride on the trails? Do you want to ride in the arena? Do you want to show your horse? Or do you just want a best friend to hang out with?

I always recommend that parents get their child an older, eight-to-fourteen-year-old, been-there-done-that type of horse, as it gives the child a best friend to talk with, to groom, and to pet—providing them with the tactile touching we all need, even in our golden years.

I grew up crying on my horse's shoulder a lot, hugging my horse, and telling my horse about the mean friends or teachers I had in school. As I matured, it changed into any other annoying person in my life. My horse would just look at me adoringly and put its head over my shoulder, which felt like a big hug, and ask for another carrot.

It was like I had my own best friend and guidance counselor who would just listen to anything I had to say without any criticism or feedback.

People have found that horses are amazing for therapeutic, emotional, and physical issues, and they excel with emotionally or physically challenged humans of all ages.

And why is this so? What is it about horses that draws us to them? Why do our little hearts turn over with joy when they nicker at us or rub their heads on us?

When you come in from being with your horse, covered in horsehair, smelling like a horse, dirt on your face and under your finger-nails, a big grin on your face, and a warm feeling in your heart, there's nothing like it.

And it's amazing how, when we spend time with horses the hours just fly by. Your spouse might remind you of that when dinner is late because you lost track of time loving on your horse.

So, as a parent, a horse is a really good babysitter for your growing children. This may also help you to realize how affordable it can be to have a horse entertain your children instead of video games, which are not physically healthy for them or good for their posture, as they sit around in a hunched-over position, using their thumbs and not getting any fresh air.

Tell your children that they need to clean stalls in order to pay for their horse's board. Then you will have them using all their muscles, exercising, and feeling a sense of self-worth for being able to earn their own horse's food, board, and keep.

Hopefully, they will dig in enthusiastically so that you are not stuck doing it, because, unfortunately, there can be quite a lot of poop to clean up from a thousand-pound grazing animal.

What do you want to do with your horse?
The best thing to do is watch some horse movies and see what lights your fire. Long trail rides? Jumping fences? Running around barrels and poles in an arena? Different breeds excel at different sports. That does not mean all breeds cannot do the sport you want to do. I have seen huge, eighteen-hand draft horses trotting around barrels in an arena for sport and fun. They will not win the timed awards though. Arabians, Morgans and Quarter horses are generally all-around horses to choose for these jobs.

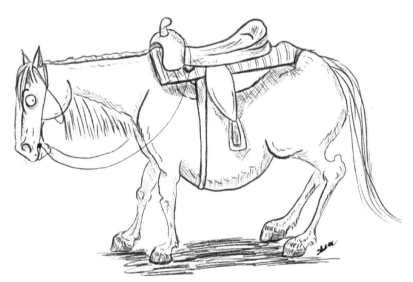

Saddles
Saddle fit is very important if you are going to be riding and training more than two days a week.

April Love

Good saddles generally start at $500. Anything you pick up under $500, you may want to have an equine professional check it over to make sure it fits your horse and that the saddle tree is not broken. A broken saddle tree would pinch the horse.

The underside of the saddle should be firm on the horse's back, so make sure it fits well. You can put the saddle on the horse's back and run your hands underneath, feeling for tight areas or gap areas.

Imagine you needed to walk to town in a pair of wooden clogs. No matter how many pads or layers of socks you put on your feet, you would not want to walk day after day if they were not comfortable. Or, imagine a backpack you are carrying with lumps pushing into your back. Well, the same applies to a horse.

I grew up riding bareback because we could never find an affordable saddle that would fit my older swayback horse. This meant that the underside of the saddle—a non-flexible form of wood covered by leather—did not fit his back well.

The horse's back moves and turns in motion, and generally, cheap saddles do not fit horses well.

In those days, I preferred riding with my bareback pad and stirrups, which was very dangerous. The girth that went underneath and around the horse to tighten the pad to his back had a buckle similar to an old car or airplane seatbelt.

There was no way to get the girth tight enough to stay in place. So, when we were running with the wind in our faces and he saw something like a rabbit to spook him, it meant that I was on my butt in the dirt and he was on his way home.

After riding for over twenty-five years, I now prefer what are called **Treeless saddles** because they conform to the horse's back and our 'sensitive derrieres.' They are much more comfortable and allow better movement for the horse.

Unfortunately, these saddles can also slide sideways. A breast collar that clips to the girth ring between their front legs and goes up in a V and clips up over the mane, just in front of the saddle, and then attaches to the D ring on the front of the saddle is a good way to keep your treeless saddle more secure.

Mounting from higher up is also best for the horse's back and the stability of the saddle, whether it's a treed or treeless saddle.

There are so many brands out there now that I wouldn't know what to recommend.

The brand I am most familiar with and like is the Bob Marshall Sport Saddle line for western-type riding. You can choose to have a horn in front of you to hold onto, which is great for racing around barrels or poles in a timed event.

The Freeform line is for those who prefer English-style riding. You have nothing to hold onto in front of you or behind you, which develops what is called 'your seat' for proper balance or squeezing your legs. Be careful with the squeezing-legs part as that is usually the signal for the horse to go faster! Not something you want to be doing if you are on your way off the horse in one of those *involuntary dismounts* we discussed earlier.

Chapter 3 - About Feeding

What are we supposed to feed these critters? And what affects how they chew?

What do you feed something that weighs between eight hundred and eighteen hundred pounds?

Remember to watch where your toes are around these magnificent creatures. No open-toed sandals please! That's a good way to get broken toes or lose a toenail.

Always wear closed-toed shoes, preferably a boot of some type with traction on the soles. Slipping and falling in winter mud or fresh manure is not a pleasant experience.

How much are they supposed to eat?
Are they supposed to eat all day? Really? Yes, that is why they are affectionately called lawn mowers. Head-down grazing on short grass is how their digestive system is designed. With their heads down, their teeth are in the proper position for grinding their feed efficiently. Feeding up from a rack is not the best for their digestion or chewing well. Head down is how they were meant to chew and digest their feeds.

Horses are meant to be grazers, meaning they tear dry brown or fresh green grass with their front teeth and chew it up with their back teeth. This usually happens as they walk and graze, so their hooves get stimulated as well.

In smaller confined areas, we feed them chopped dried grass we call hay that comes in bales. As a general rule, horses eat a certain percentage of their bodyweight, with athletic horses needing much more.

My nine-hundred-pound Arabian horses used to eat a 125-pound bale of hay in six days with added supplements since they were ridden a lot. I preferred to keep them on grasses closer to their natural diet like Orchard grass or Timothy hay and to stay away from the rich green Legume called Alfalfa, which is too high in calcium and protein for horses but used to marble fat on the meat of cows meant for butchering.

To feed grain or not to feed grain?
Grain, which has extra carbohydrates in it, is mainly meant for hard-working horses and should be limited to small amounts on their days off. Horses need nutrition for working and growing which can be provided in added supplements.

I prefer the Dynamite nutritional brand, and they have a product called Dynamite Plus, which horses love. I can feed a handful of vitamins to horses that do not need the extra carbohydrates grain provides. We used the Regular Dynamite vitamins with higher mineral content for our hard-working horses.

If you have an older horse that is having a hard time keeping weight on, the first thing you should have checked is its teeth by an equine dental professional. If they cannot chew their food well and digest it well, they cannot put on weight. The professional equine dental professional I am referring to here is not normally your local veterinarian.

The second thing to look into is a **liquid probiotic** that helps the gut flora break down the food that they are eating. Powdered probiotics just don't seem to work as well. Liquid probiotics have digestive enzymes in them that help horses utilize their feed better and help the good-gut flora thrive in their intestines. My favorite is Dynamite Dynapro which is really a pre-biotic helping good-gut flora thrive.

Soaked hay pellets in a wet mash can help as well. Sometimes older horses stop eating because they just get tired of chewing. I prefer Timothy or Orchard grass hay pellets that can be bought at local feed stores in fifty-pound bags. Oat hay would be my third choice.

I stay away from cubed pressed hay as I have a friend who fed a lot of it to her horses and then had to put down two horses because of enteroliths or 'stones,' as they are called. The chopped-pressed hay cubes she used have a binder on them to keep the hay together. Unfortunately, this also bound up other things inside the intestines.

Enteroliths are calcium or mineral buildups around a foreign substance in the horse's gut, like a piece of debris or baling twine that the horse could not digest. The body surrounds the foreign substance with the hard minerals like an oyster building a pearl. Unfortunately, the buildups keep growing over the years, creating gassy and mysterious colic's. The stones my friend had from her two horses were bigger than grapefruits and weighed over ten pounds each.

UC Davis did a study on feeding organic apple cider vinegar to horses with enteroliths and found that it did indeed help to break down the outer hard surface of the enteroliths so that they could hopefully pass out of the digestive tract. The equine dentist I used would look at the horse's fresh manure pile to see how they were breaking down their feeds.

Parasites or worms can take away from a horse's health and nutrition as well. A horse that is copper deficient will have a burnt-looking hair coat as well as pick up parasites more easily.

How do you know if your horse has worms? How often to deworm them?
You can pick up some fresh poop and drop it off at your local veterinary office. They prefer it in a Ziploc bag please. They can do a **fecal** count to see if the horse is shedding worms, as well as look for sand coming from the gut. They will also let you know what type of worms your horse may have.

April Love

Sand in the gut? How did that get there?
They can pick up sand when eating hay or spilled grain off the ground. Sometimes it is in the hay flakes as well as in the hay pellets. So, giving horses, especially in sandy areas, Psyllium once a month is a good idea. I prefer pellets which you can easily add to their feed.

There are some poisonous dewormer's sold in feed stores that are syringed into the mouth and can burn the mouth lining, as well as give the horse a sour stomach.

I prefer an all-natural organic dewormer like Diatomaceous earth, which must be of human-grade quality for the horses. I used the Dynamite Excel product in their daily feed throughout the deworming process, choosing not to use the poisonous ones, which are hard on the whole system. Oregano oil is also said to be a natural dewormer. It can be mixed with a little molasses and syringed into the mouth for seven days. If used straight, it can burn the lip lining.

We prefer to deworm on the full-moon cycle as it has been said that more worms hatch from the eggs during that cycle, so the dewormer can be more effective. Do not work your horse after deworming for a few days to let its body process the chemicals.

As far as hay and grain nowadays, there really is no nutrition or minerals left in the soil anymore. Twenty-five years ago, a horse could work hard without added supplements. Present day feeds are mostly just fillers, so added nutrition is needed. I prefer vitamins they can eat without grain like Dynamite Plus.

Your horse's teeth should be checked once a year to make sure they can grind their feed well and do not have sharp edges cutting their cheeks or tongue.

Why you ask? Did you know their teeth are not like ours? Our adult teeth come in and that is it until they deteriorate or fall out.

The adult teeth of a horse start coming in around three to four years of age, with 'caps' from the baby teeth that need to fall off or be removed by an equine dentist.

The adult teeth continue to grow up out of the gums and can become quite long. As they chew things in the wild like tough dry grasses, twigs, bark, etc. to meet their digestive and nutritional needs, they sometimes wear their teeth down.

After a horse has taken a head trauma while pulling back when tied to a post or fence, the pressure from the halter shifts and moves the cranial bones. Then the horse cannot chew correctly.

When this happens, they start chewing up and down instead of grinding sideways as they were meant to.

Sadly, most people think the horse is okay after the life-or-death struggle it went through to get away when its head was trapped. I teach all about this in my classes and free YouTube videos online.

When they start chewing up and down, it creates what is called 'hooks and waves' in the horse's teeth and sharp edges that can gouge into their cheeks and tongue. Remember what it was like when you accidentally bit your tongue or cheek? Well, try to imagine having shark-like teeth and eating your food, and continually catching your cheek. Not fun.

Most riders use a metal bit in the horse's mouth that can, when pulled on, create pain for them and their sharp teeth.

Sometimes we see things like head tossing or a horse that is hard to bridle. Such behavior is labeled as training and behavioral issues; when in reality, they are just pain issues. Once the pain issues are addressed, the horse can go back to being a happy, healthy, fun riding companion.

Also, their vision can be affected by head traumas.

And what exactly does this mean? Well, if you lift your horse's head just a little to kiss it on the nose and you look up at its eyes, you might notice that the eyes are different shapes or even pointed in different directions! This all comes from the head traumas in their past that you probably don't even know about. When people say 'they are fine' after a severe pull back, it is not a correct diagnosis, as many cranial bones have been compressed and many things have shifted.

Once you have noticed the difference in their eyes, now tilt its head down so you are looking at its forehead. A treat in your flat hand is a great way to get this done. Look at the horse's cheek bones on the side of its head and you will probably see that one side is a little lower than the other. After you see this, look down and you will see a difference in their nostrils. And then looking up, you will see that one eye is a little lower than the other, as well.

This is all the damage done from just one 'pull-back-when-tied' incident which happened when the horse was young and in training.

Head trauma damage can create a horse that spooks. What is a spook? Well, when you and the horse are going along just fine and suddenly you are not on the horse anymore because you've done another *involuntary dismount*. This happens when the horse saw something that scared it and moved faster than you could react to stay in the saddle.

I have a video on my website to teach you how to do Cranial Sacral releases on your horse yourself.

After all, this is what this book is about: how to identify the issues yourself through better knowledge and how to empower yourself to make positive changes in your horse, saving big $$ in the long run, meaning fewer x-rays from *involuntary dismounts* and fewer dental floating's of your horse's teeth.

Chapter 4 - Training and Behavioral Issues

What exactly are training and behavioral issues?
Horses have been mislabeled for decades. A horse in pain, not wanting to do what we ask, or behaving badly when being saddled has been labeled 'needs more training or has a behavioral issue that needs correcting.' And, horse owners have been sending their horses out to 'be trained to behave' at $500 to $1,000 per month, when it would have been better for the horse and for your pocketbook to find and fix the body issues creating the behavioral issues.

Sadly, when the horse is returned, it usually behaves worse than when it left, or it comes back very sore or lame. I will explain why in just a little bit.

The myth is to lunge the horse round and round in the arena or round pen until they are ready to listen to you and behave the way you want them to, whether it is causing them pain or not. You will see this in a lot of training barns as well as in natural horsemanship techniques.

If you look closely, though, for when the horse is pinning its ears or swishing its tail when worked at liberty, with no halter or ropes on them, you will see them do this when a certain way of movement is asked of them or they're asked to reverse direction. When they do this, they are letting us know it is painful to move that way, and sadly, the natural horsemanship people I have seen are not looking at this as deeply as I feel they should.

I used to retrain horses that were labeled dangerous or hard to train in just thirty days and when the owners came to pick them up, they would say, "That's not my horse. This is a calm, safe, friendly horse. What did you do with the fire-breathing dragon I dropped off here?"

"I simply listened to the horse," I said.

"Oh, you're one of those 'horse whisperers'?"

And I would say, "No, I listened to what the horse needed, fixed the body issues causing the pain, got an equine dentist in to float their teeth, and balanced the hooves so they could move correctly and their joints could move painlessly. When the horse comes back to joy, comfort, and ease in its body, then it is very happy to do for me what I am asking of it."

When a horse is in pain and not happy, it will act up, just as you would if you had to do physical work that was causing you great pain. They are letting you know they are in pain somewhere. I have videos on my website that teach you how to find and release the issues yourself. They are for beginners! Believe it or not!

If you are not ready to dive into all this, then I recommend having a horse chiropractor or equine bodywork professional check your horse out before getting mad at the horse for bad behavior under saddle.

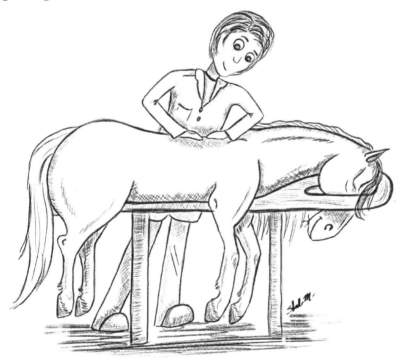

You are looking for more than an equine masseuse. One problem is that there are quite a few modalities out there that are just treating the symptoms and not looking for or working on the cause of the pain. What does that mean?

Well, if you had shoes that the outside edge was worn down and when you went hiking, and your foot could not land properly, by the end of the day your calves would be sore and the following day they would be tight and painful. Well, that's how the horse's legs feel after working on hooves not in balance.

Now imagine that your right shoulder is not working well and is stiff. Then you are asked to garden and pull weeds or paint the ceiling all day. You would get more sore, tired, and cranky by the end of the day. Imagine that you had to go back five days in a row and do the same thing over and over. This is what is happening when a horse is in training and being lunged five days a week. You would not be comfortable and probably be cranky when someone asked you to do it over again and again, five days a week. You would probably want to quit!

Well, these are our horses when their first rib is out of alignment and it doesn't allow the side shoulder on that side to move correctly. So, they do not want to canter around on that lead. If the first rib right side is not where it should be, it causes right shoulder issues, and they would not want to canter to the right in the round pen.

Sadly, we have been misinformed that this is a weakness or training issue, and the horse is asked to do more of it until they have the right attitude about it.

I cringe every time I see that. My hope is that people will become better informed and will learn to fix the cause that is creating the 'training and behavior issues', as well as 'mysterious lameness'.

All this misalignment pulls the withers, mid-ribs, and pelvis out of alignment, and you will have a crooked horse.

You might get one or two good rides from your horse. Then, it will seem to get crankier; pinning its ears back or swishing its tail when you are tightening the girth. When you tighten the girth of a hard symmetrical-shaped saddle on a non-symmetrical-shaped horse's body, it works against the horse in motion and causes the horse pain.

Stand on a bucket about ten feet behind your horse and look at the shape of its back. On the rump you will see one side more muscled or higher. You will see one side rib usually lower, one shoulder bigger, and the withers—where the mane ends near the back—not straight either. Yet this horse will pass a pre-purchase exam done by an equine professional.

Now squat down ten feet behind the horse, if it is safe to do so, and look at the back of the hooves. You will see different shapes and some areas of the hoof will be higher or lower, and not round like they should be.

So now you see your horse is not symmetrical; neither are the hooves it stands on. This creates a body not loading the joints correctly and premature arthritic conditions. Mysterious lameness starts to show up usually before they are even ten years old, but really, they're not mysterious lameness.

You can learn the cause of your horse's pain and how to work on all these issues yourself at home. I and my certified instructors are just an email, skype, or call away whenever you need help.

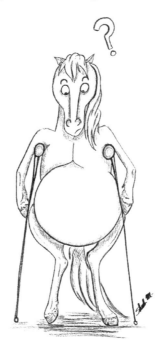

The big problem here is that the area that is sore is not necessarily where the lameness originated.

The area that is sore is where the body was overworked; compensating for an area or body part that was originally unable to do its job properly.

Watch their ears, tail, and body when you do something with them. They will tell you a story. Watch someone riding in an arena and when they ask their horse to do something different. Notice if the ears move back or pin flat back and the tail swishes in agitation.

When you put a saddle pad and saddle on your horse, do any of these telltale signs happen?

When you start to tighten the girth, is your horse happily dozing?

Or bracing, shaking its withers or skin like to rid itself of pesky flies or biting or clenching its jaw or swishing its tail?

All signs of extreme agitation and discomfort.

Adding our weight in the saddle on top of that creates more discomfort, which can create issues like bucking, walking off while trying to mount, biting at stirrups, not wanting to canter, or change leads or diagonal.

These are not training issues. These are body issues that need to be corrected so both the horse and rider can enjoy the time spent riding together, and so the horse can be rideable into its 30's.

Right about the time a horse has a calm enough personality and demeanor to be safe for your family, they start breaking down. What can you do about this?

Yes, **you** can learn some simple things that I and my certified instructors teach to help your horse become a happy, loyal horse—drama and accident free.

Also having an equine dentist, with many years of experience—not customarily your local veterinarian—check your horse's mouth and teeth for sharp edges and dental issues, will give you a happy horse lasting well into its 30's.

On my website (www.holistichorseworks.com), I have many self-help videos. I also offer long-distance readings to dial down on your horse's issues. You get a six-page PDF report of what is going on in your horse's body—including environmental, bacterial, viral, muscular, skeletal, and cranial issues. Where your horse has pain and what you can do to help your horse.

I also have certified instructors around the world from whom you can take classes.

Ready for more? Look for the next book in this series Horse 102.

About the Author

April Love (formerly April Battles) is renown in the world of equine bodywork for her unique techniques in working with horses and teaches nationally and internationally.

She teaches horse owners how observe their horses and interpret their behavior in order to determine their problems, and then how to help correct their them.

She has many DVDs and free videos to educate, inform, and assist horse owners in resolving their horses' problems themselves. This list is included in the front of this book.

Many of her students who have recognized the benefits of April's unique techniques have become practitioners and certified instructors, globally and they are listed on her website.

This is just a brief introduction to April Love. To learn more about her personally, her classes, and her recommended products, and to read testimonies from people she has helped, go to her website: www.holistichorseworks.com.
Email: april @holistichorseworks.com
Phone: (530) 823-7321 HST

April Love

- Certified instructor for Quantum Relief for horses and humans
- Certified instructor for Ting Point Therapy
- Access Consciousness practitioner – break the negative patterns that keep repeating in your life
- Osteopathy for Deep Myofascial muscular and skeletal releases
- Cranio Sacral and Massage Therapy
- Bio-Energy Therapy
- Equine Kinesiology
- Nutritional Therapy
- Acupressure and Reiki
- Unwinding the whole horse for the body, mind, heart and soul

Remember life without pain?

- Release the soft tissues
- Flush emotional traumas
- Remove defensive habits
- Correct nutritional imbalances
- Balance the energetic system

April Love

Blank page to write some notes about your horse

Made in the USA
Las Vegas, NV
20 January 2021